JR. GRAPHIC AMERICAN INVENTORS

HENRY FORD

FORD PIQUETTE PLANT

Steven Roberts

PowerKiDS press.

New York

Published in 2013 by The Rosen Publishing Group, Inc.
29 East 21st Street, New York, NY 10010

First Edition

Editor: Joanne Randolph

Book Design: Planman Technologies

Illustrations: Planman Technologies

Library of Congress Cataloging-in-Publication Data

Roberts, Steven, 1955–

Henry Ford / by Steven Roberts. — 1st ed.

  p. cm. — (Jr. graphic American inventors)

Includes index.

ISBN 978-1-4777-0079-2 (library binding) — ISBN 978-1-4777-0143-0 (pbk.) — ISBN 978-1-4777-0144-7 (6-pack)

1. Ford, Henry, 1863-1947-Juvenile literature. 2. Automobile industry and trade-United States—Biography—Juvenile literature. 3. Industrialists-United States-Biography -Juvenile literature. I. Title.

TL140.F6R63 2013

338.7'629222092-dc23

[B]

2012020485

Manufactured in the United States of America

CPSIA Compliance Information: Batch # W13PK1: For Further Information contact Rosen Publishing, New York, New York at 1-800-237-9932

Contents

Introduction

Henry Ford founded the Ford Motor Company, one of the largest **automakers** in the world. He used the modern **assembly line** to make the first **mass-produced automobile**. His car the Model T changed the way we work and live.

Main Characters

Thomas Edison (1847–1931) Famous American inventor who employed Henry Ford.

Clara Bryant Ford (1866–1950) Wife of Henry Ford.

Edsel Ford (1893–1943) Son and only child of Henry Ford. He became president of the Ford Motor Company.

Henry Ford (1863–1947) American engineer, inventor, and businessman.

William H. Murphy (c. 1800s) Early business partner of Henry Ford.

Barney Oldfield (1878–1946) American bicycle racer who became a famous racecar driver.

HENRY FORD

TODAY'S LESSON IS ON **AGRICULTURE**.

HENRY FORD WAS BORN IN 1863 IN DEARBORN, MICHIGAN, NEAR THE CITY OF DETROIT. HE WAS THE OLDEST OF SIX CHILDREN AND WENT TO SCHOOL IN A ONE-ROOM SCHOOLHOUSE.

GROWING WHEAT

Dearborn

Michigan

WHEN HE WASN'T ATTENDING SCHOOL, HENRY FORD WORKED ON HIS FATHER'S FARM.

HENRY WAS VERY INTERESTED IN THE FARM MACHINERY. HE LIKED FIGURING OUT HOW THE MACHINES WORKED.

COME ON, HENRY. WE HAVE TO GO WORK IN THE FIELDS.

WHEN HE WAS 13, HIS FATHER GAVE HIM A WATCH. HENRY LEARNED HOW TO TAKE IT APART AND PUT IT BACK TOGETHER AGAIN.

DO YOU THINK YOU CAN FIX IT?

BEFORE LONG, THE NEIGHBORS WERE GIVING HENRY THEIR BROKEN WATCHES TO FIX.

YES, IT WILL BE READY IN A DAY OR TWO.

WHEN HE WAS 16, HENRY LEFT HOME AND WENT TO NEARBY DETROIT TO FIND WORK. HE BECAME AN **APPRENTICE MACHINIST** AT THE DETROIT DRY DOCK COMPANY, WHICH MADE **STEAM ENGINES** FOR SHIPS.

THE FORCE OF THE STEAM IS WHAT DRIVES THE ENGINE.

HENRY FORD LATER WENT TO WORK FOR THE WESTINGHOUSE ELECTRIC CORPORATION. HIS JOB WAS REPAIRING ENGINES.

GOOD WORK, HENRY. IT LOOKS LIKE YOU REALLY KNOW WHAT YOU'RE DOING!

HENRY, IT LOOKS AS GOOD AS NEW.

AFTER THREE YEARS IN DETROIT, HENRY FORD MOVED BACK TO THE FAMILY FARM TO HELP HIS FATHER. HE REPAIRED FARM EQUIPMENT WHILE CONTINUING TO WORK IN DETROIT.

IN 1888, FORD MARRIED CLARA BRYANT. HE MOVED TO A FARM OF HIS OWN AND GOT A JOB RUNNING A **SAWMILL**.

JUST ONE MORE ORDER TO FILL TODAY!

IN 1891, THE EDISON ILLUMINATING COMPANY, IN DETROIT, HIRED FORD AS AN ENGINEER. THOMAS EDISON HAD FOUNDED THE COMPANY.

IN 1893, FORD'S SON, EDSEL, WAS BORN. HE WOULD BE HENRY AND CLARA'S ONLY CHILD.

SON, I BROUGHT YOU A PRESENT.

THAT SAME YEAR, FORD WAS PROMOTED TO CHIEF ENGINEER AT THE EDISON COMPANY. THIS GAVE HIM ENOUGH TIME AND MONEY TO WORK ON HIS OWN ENGINES.

FORD SHOWED HIS FIRST **INTERNAL COMBUSTION ENGINE** TO HIS WIFE CLARA ON CHRISTMAS EVE IN 1893.

IT WORKS!

I WANT MY ENGINE TO MOVE PEOPLE IN A **CARRIAGE.**

FORD WORKED HARD TO DEVELOP A HORSELESS CARRIAGE, OR AUTOMOBILE. FORD EXPERIMENTED WITH DIFFERENT DESIGNS USING CHAINS, BICYCLE TIRES, AND LEVERS FOR TWO YEARS.

FINALLY, IN 1896, FORD COMPLETED HIS FIRST AUTOMOBILE. HE CALLED IT THE **QUADRICYCLE**, WHICH MEANS "FOUR WHEELS." IT COULD GO 20 MILES PER HOUR (32 KM/H).

SO WHAT DO YOU THINK?

WHAT FUN!

IN JUNE 1896, FORD DROVE HIS QUADRICYCLE FOR THE FIRST TIME THROUGH THE STREETS OF DETROIT, MICHIGAN.

WOW, WHAT'S THAT?

HOW DOES IT WORK?

FORD SHOWED HIS INVENTION TO HIS BOSS, THOMAS EDISON. EDISON ENCOURAGED FORD TO KEEPING WORKING ON HIS QUADRICYCLE, SO HE BUILT A NEW MODEL.

IN 1899, FORD FOUNDED THE DETROIT AUTOMOBILE COMPANY WITH SOME INVESTORS. HIS BIGGEST INVESTOR WAS WILLIAM H. MURPHY, A LUMBER **TYCOON**.

THE COMPANY'S PRODUCTS COST TOO MUCH TO MAKE AND WERE TOO EXPENSIVE. IN ABOUT A YEAR, THE COMPANY WENT OUT OF BUSINESS.

FORD DESIGNED AND BUILT RACING CARS, WHICH HE RACED HIMSELF. THESE CARS ATTRACTED NEW INVESTORS.

IN 1901, THE HENRY FORD COMPANY WAS FORMED. MURPHY CONTROLLED THE COMPANY, AND FORD WAS ITS CHIEF ENGINEER.

WE HAVE TO MAKE CARS FASTER AND CHEAPER!

I QUIT!

I RUN THIS COMPANY, NOT YOU!

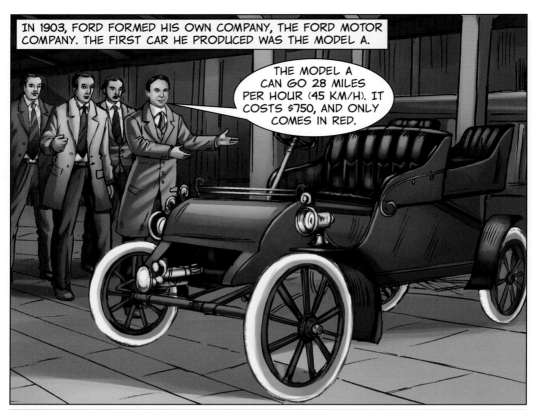

IN 1903, FORD FORMED HIS OWN COMPANY, THE FORD MOTOR COMPANY. THE FIRST CAR HE PRODUCED WAS THE MODEL A.

THE MODEL A CAN GO 28 MILES PER HOUR (45 KM/H). IT COSTS $750, AND ONLY COMES IN RED.

THE MODEL C AND THEN THE MODEL F FOLLOWED THE MODEL A.

TO PROMOTE HIS COMPANY, FORD BUILT A SPECIAL RACING CAR. HE ASKED BARNEY OLDFIELD, A 24-YEAR-OLD BICYCLE RACER, TO DRIVE IT.

DO YOU THINK YOU CAN DRIVE IT?

I'LL GIVE IT A TRY.

OLDFIELD NAMED THE CAR THE 999. HE BEGAN TO WIN RACES AND SET SPEED RECORDS. HE HELPED MAKE THE FORD MOTOR COMPANY FAMOUS.

THE NEWS

BARNEY OLDFIELD WINS AGAIN!!"

FORD AND OLDFIELD HELPED MAKE THE SPORT OF AUTO RACING POPULAR. BARNEY OLDFIELD BECAME THE MOST FAMOUS RACECAR DRIVER IN THE COUNTRY.

IN 1907, FORD ANNOUNCED A NEW PLAN FOR THE COMPANY. HE WANTED TO PRODUCE A CAR THAT EVERYONE COULD AFFORD.

THIS CAR WILL BE EASY TO MAKE, EASY TO DRIVE, EASY TO FIX, AND IT WILL BE AFFORDABLE.

FORD PIQUETTE PLANT

THE CAR FORD INTRODUCED IN 1908 WAS THE MODEL T. IT WAS A **REVOLUTION** IN AUTO MAKING AND CHANGED THE AMERICAN WAY OF LIFE.

FORD'S MODEL T COST $825, COULD GO 30 MILES PER HOUR (48 KM/H), AND CAME IN ONLY ONE COLOR, BLACK.

FORD SET UP CAR DEALERSHIPS THROUGHOUT THE UNITED STATES AND ADVERTISED THE MODEL T. IT SOON BECAME THE BEST-SELLING CAR IN THE COUNTRY.

THIS IS THE CAR OF THE FUTURE!

THE MODEL T WAS SO SUCCESSFUL THAT FORD COULDN'T MAKE THE CARS FAST ENOUGH. THEY WERE STILL MADE BY TEAMS OF WORKERS PUTTING TOGETHER ONE CAR AT A TIME.

HURRY UP. WE STILL HAVE TO MAKE FOUR MORE TODAY.

FORD WENT TO OTHER TYPES OF FACTORIES TO SEE HOW THEY MADE THINGS. AT A MEATPACKING PLANT, HE SAW HOW THE PRODUCT MOVED ALONG A **CONVEYOR BELT**.

AT A SEWING MACHINE FACTORY, FORD SAW HOW EACH WORKER PUT TOGETHER ONLY ONE PIECE OF A SEWING MACHINE.

FORD DECIDED TO USE THESE IDEAS ON A NEW ASSEMBLY LINE. WORKERS BEGAN TO MAKE CARS MUCH FASTER BECAUSE THE PARTS MOVED ALONG A CONVEYOR BELT. EACH WORKER WORKED ON JUST ONE PART OF THE CAR.

WITHIN A FEW YEARS, FORD WAS MAKING ONE MILLION MODEL Ts EACH YEAR. BY 1918, HALF OF ALL THE CARS IN THE UNITED STATES WERE MODEL Ts.

FORD HAD A NEW PROBLEM. WORKING ON AN ASSEMBLY LINE WAS BORING, AND THE WORKDAY WAS LONG. AS A RESULT, WORKERS OFTEN QUIT.

WE WON'T MAKE OUR PRODUCTION QUOTA TODAY.

THREE MORE WORKERS QUIT YESTERDAY.

I HEAR THIS IS A GREAT PLACE TO WORK.

FORD CAME UP WITH OTHER IDEAS TO KEEP HIS WORKERS FROM LEAVING. HE INCREASED THEIR WAGES. HE INTRODUCED A 40-HOUR WORKWEEK, STILL FOLLOWED BY MANY COMPANIES TODAY.

IN 1927, FORD MADE HIS LAST MODEL T. BY THEN, HE HAD MADE MORE THAN 15 MILLION OF THEM.

IT IS THE END OF AN ERA.

IN 1928, FORD OPENED A NEW FACTORY ON THE BANKS OF THE ROUGE RIVER, IN MICHIGAN. IT WAS THE LARGEST FACTORY IN THE WORLD.

HENRY FORD'S SON, EDSEL, BECAME PRESIDENT OF FORD MOTOR COMPANY. HENRY AND EDSEL OFTEN DISAGREED ON HOW TO RUN THE COMPANY.

FATHER, WE HAVE TO MODERNIZE! OUR CARS NEED A NEW LOOK AND NEW FEATURES.

I'LL MAKE THOSE DECISIONS!

IN 1928, FORD CAME OUT WITH A NEW MODEL A. HENRY AND EDSEL WORKED TOGETHER TO DEVELOP IT. FORD CAME OUT WITH NEW MODELS EVERY YEAR, LIKE THE MODEL B.

IN 1937, ORGANIZERS TRIED TO GET FORD WORKERS TO JOIN A **LABOR UNION**. THE UNION WANTED BETTER PAY AND WORKING CONDITIONS.

HENRY FORD HIRED MEN TO BREAK UP THE STRIKE. THE COMPANY AND THE UNION FOUGHT IN WHAT BECAME KNOWN AS THE BATTLE OF THE OVERPASS.

IN 1938, HENRY FORD BECAME ILL AND RETIRED FROM THE COMPANY.

CAN I GET YOU ANYTHING, FATHER?

JUST MAKE SURE TO TAKE CARE OF THE COMPANY!

WHEN EDSEL DIED IN 1943, HENRY FORD CAME OUT OF RETIREMENT TO RUN THE COMPANY AGAIN. BY THEN, HE WAS OLD AND FRAIL.

HENRY FORD DIED IN 1947. HE DID NOT INVENT THE AUTOMOBILE OR THE ASSEMBLY LINE, BUT HE USED THEM TO MAKE CARS THAT EVERYONE COULD OWN.

21

Timeline

1863   Henry Ford is born on July 30 near the city of Detroit, Michigan.

1879   Ford leaves home to work in Detroit as a machinist.

1888   Ford marries Clara Bryant. He buys his own farm and gets a job running a sawmill.

1891   The Edison Illuminating Company hires Ford as an engineer.

1893   Edsel Ford, Henry Ford's only child, is born on November 6.

1896   Ford builds his first automobile, the Quadricycle.

1899   Ford starts his first company with investors, the Detroit Automobile Company, which fails.

1901   Ford starts his second company, the Henry Ford Company, which he later quits.

1903   The Ford Motor Company is formed on June 16.

1908   On August 12, the Ford Motor Company begins making the Model T.

1913   Ford starts using the assembly line.

1918   The Model T becomes the best-selling car in the world.

1927   The last Model T is made.

1928   The Rouge River factory opens.

1937   Conflict breaks out between union organizers from the United Auto Workers and Ford's hired guards.

1938   Ford retires after suffering from an illness.

1941   The Ford Motor Company signs its first contract with the United Auto Workers.

1943   Edsel Ford dies at the age of 49. Henry Ford comes out of retirement to run the company.

1947   Henry Ford dies on April 7 at the age of 83.

Glossary

agriculture (A-grih-kul-cher) The science of producing crops and raising livestock, or animals.

apprentice (uh-PREN-tis) A person who learns a trade by working for someone who is already trained.

assembly line (uh-SEM-blee LYN) A system of workers and machines designed to mass produce products.

automakers (AW-toh-may-kerz) Companies that make automobiles.

automobile (AW-tuh-moh-beel) A vehicle designed for passengers that usually has four wheels and an internal combustion engine.

carriage (KAR-ij) A wheeled object used to carry people or things.

conveyor belt (kun-VAY-er BELT) A powered chain or belt that carries machine parts or other objects.

internal combustion engine (in-TUR-nel kum-BUS-chun EN-jin) A machine inside a car or airplane that makes the car or airplane move.

labor union (LAY-ber YOON-yun) A group of workers joined together to gain better wages and working conditions.

machinist (muh-SHEE-nist) A worker who makes, repairs, or operates manufacturing machines.

mass-produced (mas-pruh-DOOSD) Made in large amounts.

Quadricycle (KWAHD-ruh-sy-kul) The first car developed by Henry Ford.

revolution (reh-vuh-LOO-shun) A complete change.

sawmill (SAW-mil) A building in which logs are sawed into boards.

steam engines (STEEM EN-junz) Engines powered by steam.

tycoon (ty-KOON) A powerful and influential business person.

Index

A

assembly line, 3, 17, 18, 21

B

Battle of the Overpass, 20

D

Dearborn, Michigan, 4

Detroit Automobile
Company, 10

Detroit, Michigan, 4, 6, 7, 9, 10

E

Edison Company, 7, 8, 10

Edison, Thomas, 3, 10

F

Ford, Clara Bryant, 3, 7, 8, 9

Ford, Edsel, 3, 7, 9, 19, 21

Ford Motor Company, 12, 13, 14,
18, 19, 20

M

Model T, 14, 15, 17, 18

Murphy, William H., 3, 10, 11

O

Oldfield, Barney, 3, 13

Q

Quadricycle, 9, 10

W

Westinghouse Electric
Corporation, 6

Websites

Due to the changing nature of Internet links, PowerKids Press has developed an online list of websites related to the subject of this book. This site is updated regularly. Please use this link to access the list:

www.powerkidslinks.com/jgai/ford/